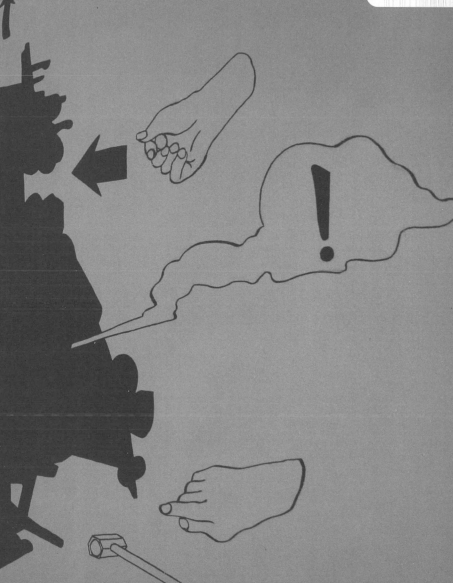

PLEASE MIND YOUR HANDS IN THE PRESS ROOM

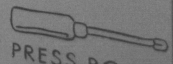

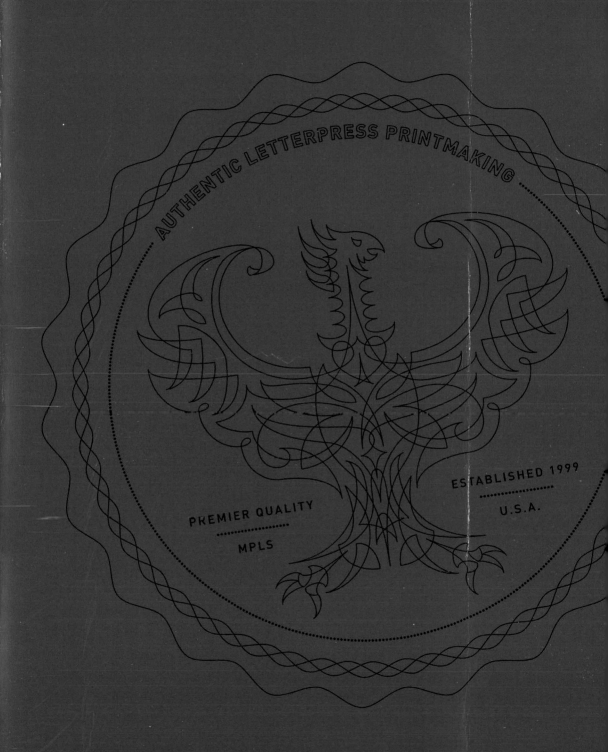

AUTHENTIC LETTERPRESS PRINTMAKING

ESTABLISHED 1999

U.S.A.

PREMIER QUALITY

MPLS

gestalten

THIS IS MY PRINTING PRESS.
THERE ARE MANY LIKE IT,
        BUT THIS ONE IS MINE.
MY PRESS IS MY BEST FRIEND.
            IT IS MY LIFE.
I MUST MASTER IT
AS I MUST MASTER MY LIFE.
    MY PRESS, WITHOUT ME, IS USELESS.
    WITHOUT MY PRESS, I AM USELESS.
I MUST INK MY PRESS TRUE.
I MUST PRINT MORE BEAUTIFULLY
        THAN NEW TECHNOLOGY THAT IS
TRYING TO KILL ME.
        I MUST INK THEM
            BEFORE THEY PIXELATE ME.
    I WILL ...

MY PRESS AND MYSELF KNOW
THAT WHAT COUNTS IN THIS PRESSROOM
IS NOT THE PAPER WE CHOOSE,
    THE PLATES WE MAKE, THE INK WE MIX,
   NOR THE BITE OF OUR IMPRESSION.
WE KNOW THAT IT IS THE SUM OF THESE
                IN PRINTING THAT COUNTS.
      WE WILL PRINT ...

In an act of rebellion I bought my first press in 1999.

I was missing something in my career as a graphic designer, having graduated in 1998 from the College of Visual Arts with a four-year BFA degree that put me through a fine arts spin cycle. College learning was a broad survey of the arts including painting, drawing, photography and sculpture, the last of which I nearly chose as my major. However, my financial sensibility prevailed and I ultimately chose a major in Communication Design.

My first design job held the usual drudge of long days in front of a computer. It was creative, yet so unlike my college experience, and while I enjoyed design, there was a distinct absence of physicality to the process. I missed making things by hand. Therefore, putting a letter-press in my basement seemed like a natural thing to do. This early base-ment studio stationed my Chandler & Price platen press between the boiler and the clothes dryer and just a step away from the cat pan. Printing in this rudimentary setup

was the purest form of experiential learning. Fast-forward a decade— that basement hobby is now a truly unique commercial printshop with a battery of Heidelberg presses and a crew of talented people.

I can credit my college experience, studying original masters like William Morris, W.A. Dwiggins, and Fredrick Goudy as contributing to my passion for letterpress printing. These fellows truly understood and merged both design and production. Today, fewer and fewer designers understand the production

methods beyond the keyboard. We have so many options that we've become generalists. At Studio On Fire, design and letterpress are merged once again. Understanding our niche letterpress market and offering production advice to the designers that come to us allows us to excel in our industry. Blending design intent with letterpress printing keeps our work exciting. Speaking as both a designer and letterpress printer for the past decade, I feel it is safe to say letterpress is still gaining momentum as a production method. When people receive a letterpress printed business card and turn it over in their hand, they feel it, look at it closer, and consider it. It literally buys time in their hands. It is this notable pause that exemplifies letterpress printing as a breath of fresh air. As our culture increases its reliance on digital communications—inclusive of the time we spend in front of glowing screens, letterpress printing becomes an even more unique counterpoint that allows us to connect with a piece of communication in real life.

It is something we both see *and* feel. Our studio works hard to make beautifully produced objects that are inspirational to those who interact with them. In our design services, we are committed to making distinctive work that engages the senses. In our printing, we are committed to making letterpress one of the most premium and relevant production methods for contemporary design. We hope you enjoy this compilation of studio designed projects and client designed projects, all printed in our Minneapolis space.

studioonfire.com

beastpieces.com

NUMBERS@STUDIOONFIRE.COM

MPLS MINNESOTA USA • NUMBERS@STUDIOONFIRE.COM • STUDIO ON FIRE
CUSTOM LETTERPRESS PRINTING — THROWING DOWN INK, HARD AND FAST • 612 379 3000

RIP

T OPERATE WHILE INTOXICATED

Paper Saw Blade Business Cards

Client & Design Firm
Studio On Fire

Belmont Associates Identity

Client
Belmont Associates

Design Firm
Studio On Fire

10 Zing Business Cards

Client
10 Zing Consulting

Design Firm
Studio On Fire

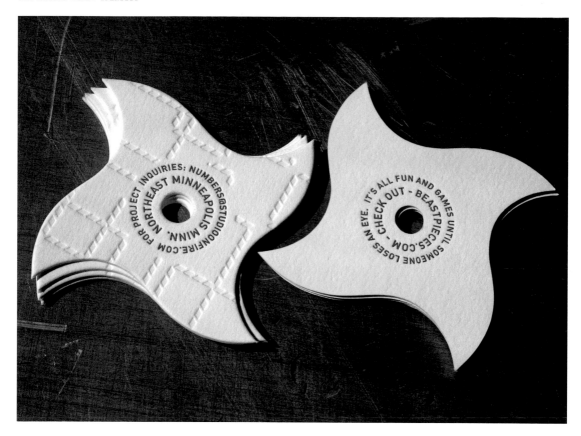

Ninja Business Cards

Client & Design Firm
Studio On Fire

Many Fold Farm Business Cards

Client
Many Fold Farm

Design Firm
Studio On Fire

Falling Deer Business Cards

Client
Carl Richetti

Design Firm
Studio On Fire

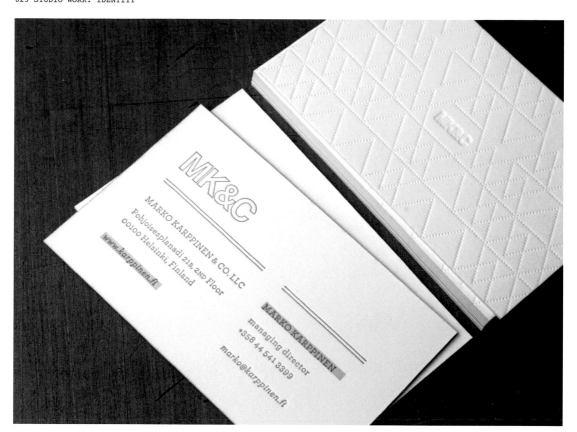

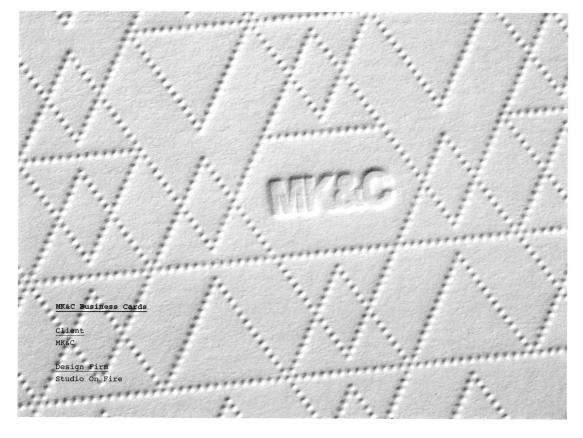

MK&C Business Cards

Client
MK&C

Design Firm
Studio On Fire

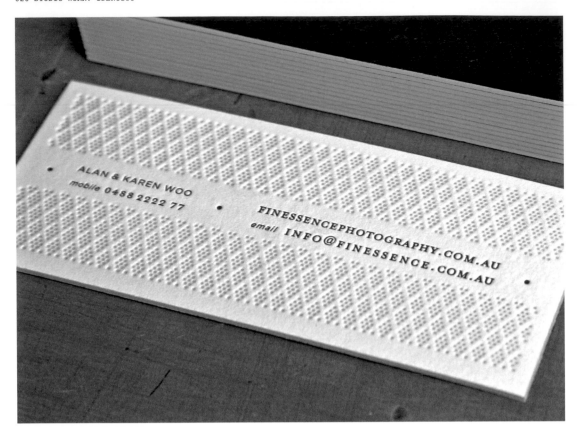

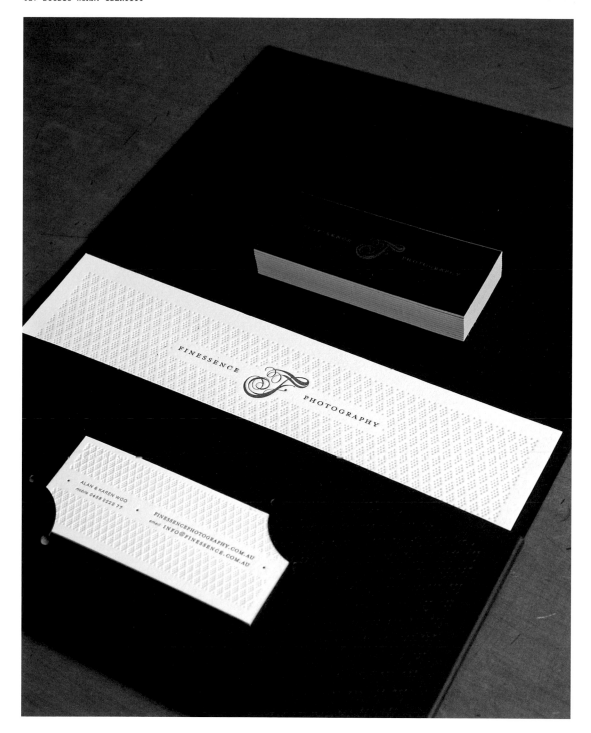

Finessence Photography Identity

Client
Finessence Photography

Design Firm
Studio On Fire

Vista Caballo Identity

Client
Vista Caballo

Copywriting
Lisa Arie

Design Firm
Studio On Fire

Creative Direction
Thinktopia

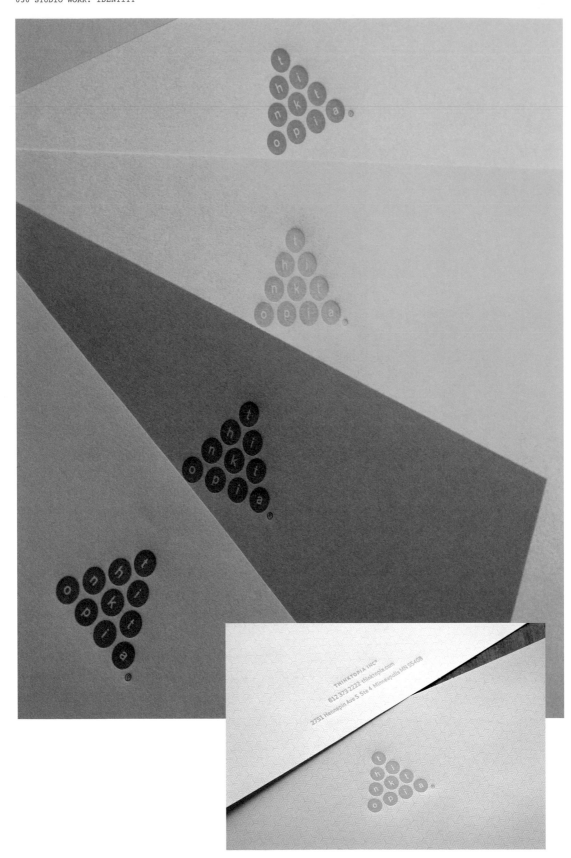

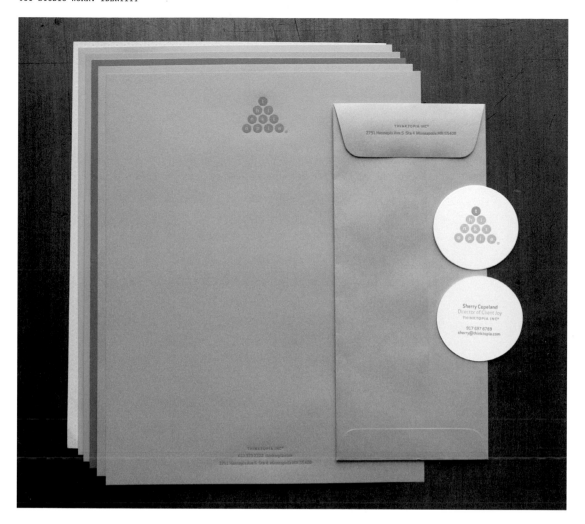

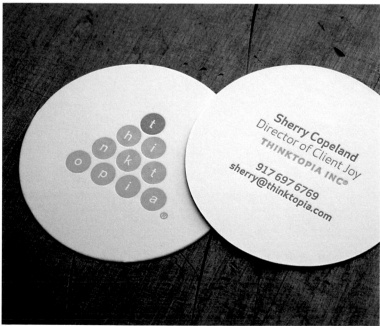

Thinktopia Stationary

Client
Thinktopia

Design Firm
Studio On Fire

Creative Direction
Patrick Hanlon

Art Direction
Paul Asao, Brian Williams,
Patrick Hanlon, Ben Levitz

Copywriting
Patrick Hanlon

space150 version 16

Client
space150

Design Firm
Studio On Fire

space150 version 17

Client
space150

Design Firm
Studio On Fire

Studio On Fire Padded Mailer
and Business Card Boxes

Design Firm
Studio On Fire

Matchbook Wedding Suite

Client
Martha Stewart
Weddings Blog

Design Firm
Studio On Fire

Telegram Wedding Suite

Client
Michelle & Bradley

Design Firm
Studio On Fire

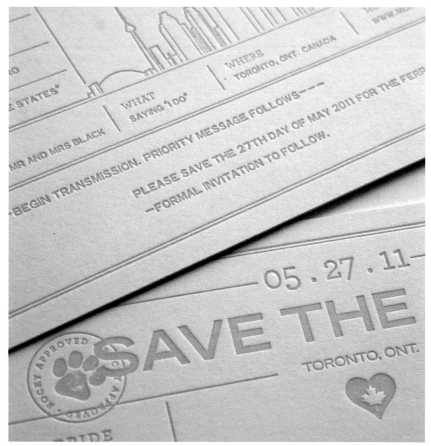

Beer Coaster Wedding Suite

Client
Katie & Josh

Design Firm
Studio On Fire

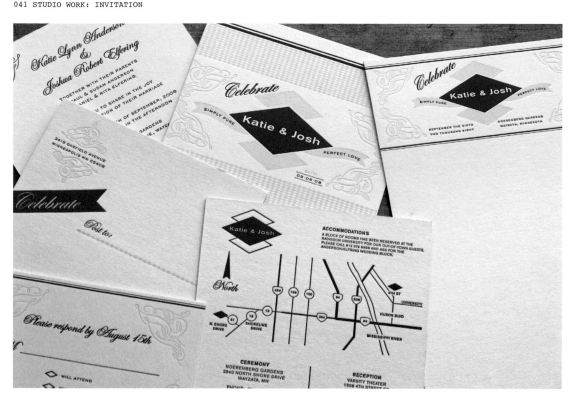

Acompañanos a festejar con
alegria, risas, amistad & amor
- LA UNIÓN MATRIMONIAL DE -

Sarah Cary
Hanson
y
Sergio René
Salgado

Bilingual Wedding Suite

Client
Sarah & Sergio

Design Firm
Studio On Fire

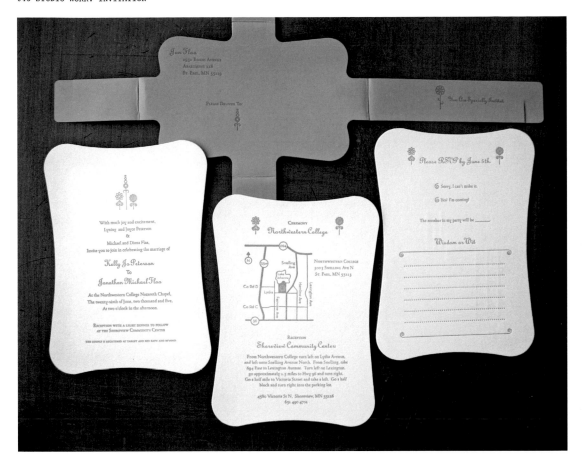

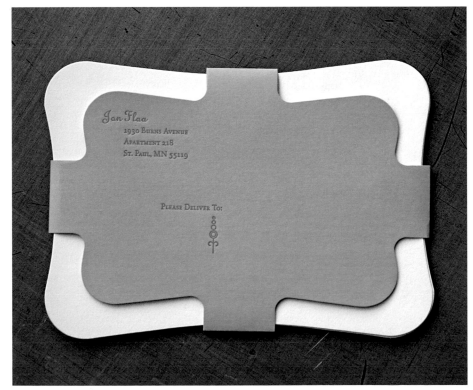

**Buckle
Wedding Suite**

Client
Kelly & Jon

Design Firm
Studio On Fire

Steven Heller
& 365: AIGA Invite

Client
College of
Visual Arts

Design Firm
Studio On Fire

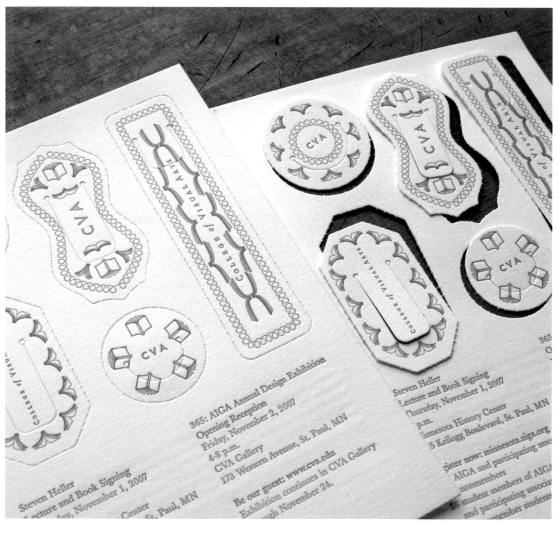

Viking Wedding

Client
Jan & Danielle

Design Firm
Studio On Fire

Cheer

Design Firm
Studio On Fire

AIGA Minnesota Design Camp 2008
Event and Promotional Materials

Client
AIGA Minnesota

Design Firm
Studio On Fire

Illustration
Jenna Brouse

American B

1971.1

t Horned Spotted Barn Beaver

Spotted Barn Beaver is an

ure with a vast wing

Native to Niawa,

fact, the

ened

Design & Letterpress:
studioonfire.com

AIGA
MINNESOTA
2008
DESIGN CAMP

Erik Brandt: Sometimes CD

<u>Client</u>
Erik Brandt

<u>Design Firm</u>
Studio On Fire

89.3 The Current™ | Live Current™ Volume Two
1   Sia / Breathe Me
2   P.O.S. / P.O.S. Is Ruining My Life
3   Amos Lee / Keep It Loose, Keep It Tight
4   Brandi Carlile / What Can I Say
5   Drive-By Truckers / Easy On Yourself
6   The Walkmen / Another One Goes By
7   James Hunter / People Gonna Talk
8   Atmosphere / Smart Went Crazy
9   The BellRays / Tell The Lie
10 The Alarmists / Some Things Never Stop
11 Gomez / Girlshapedlovedrug
12 Spoon / They Never Got You
13 The Hold Steady / Stuck Between Stations
14 Editors / Munich
15 Mates of State / Goods (All In Your Head)
16 Los Amigos Invisibles / All Day Today

89.3
the current™

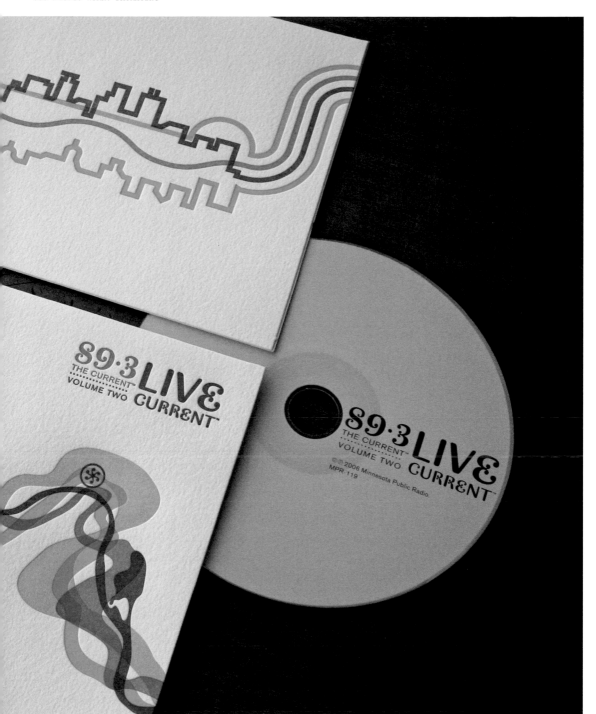

Live Current Volume Two CD

Client
Minnesota Public Radio

Design Firm
Studio On Fire

Erik Brandt: Amelia's Boot CD

Client
Erik Brandt

Design Firm
Studio On Fire

Sakura Bloom Identity and Packaging

Client
Sakura Bloom

Design Firm
Studio On Fire

Iron Beast Print

Client & Design Firm
Studio On Fire

Design Firm
Studio On Fire

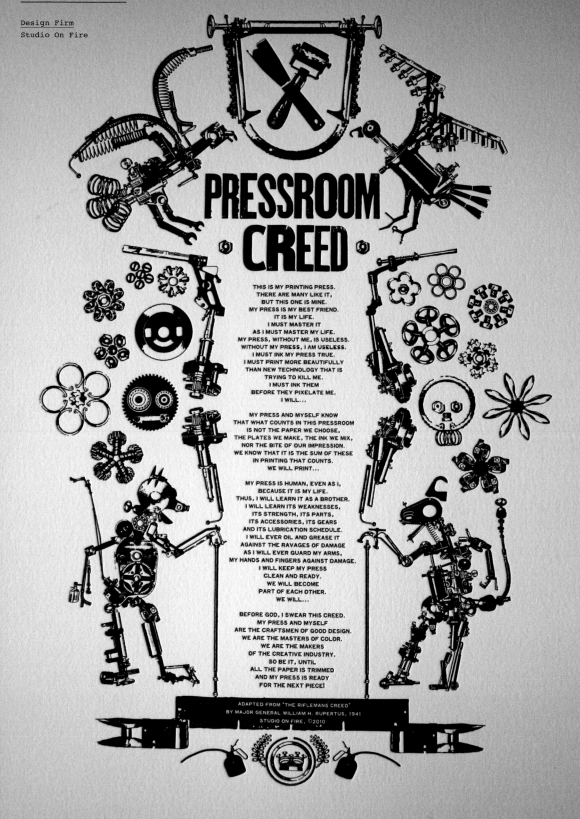

Godspeed Poster

Client & Design Firm
Studio On Fire

Wild Air Poster

Client & Design Firm
Studio On Fire

In the sunshine swing the sea drink the wild air

Excerpt from Ralph Waldo Emerson
Considerations by the Way, 1860

Studio On Fire   50 / 150

Birds of Sadness Poster

Client & Design Firm
Studio On Fire

Golden Rule Poster

Client & Design Firm
Studio On Fire

Type & Illustration / Kora, Age 8
Design / Studio On Fire

Feast Mpls Poster

Client
Feast Minneapolis

Design Firm
Studio On Fire

Design
David Dresbach

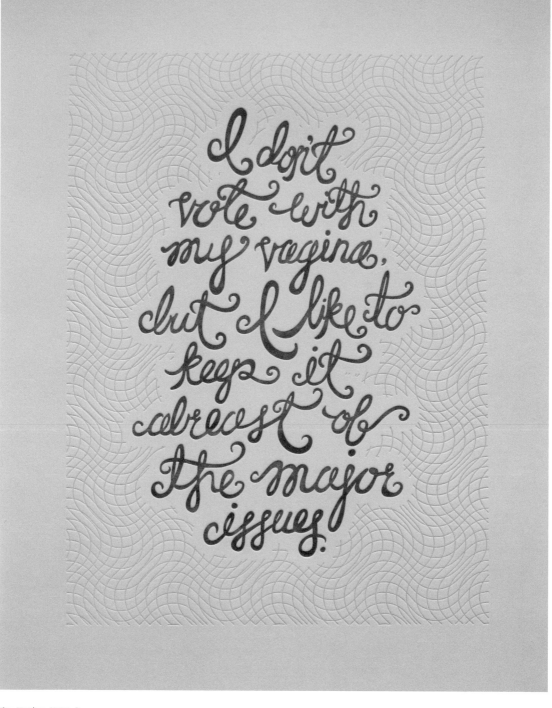

The Vagina Vote 2

Client
Poster Offensive 2010

Design Firm
Studio On Fire

Design
Samantha Michaels

Visual Poster,
Version 1

Client
College of Visual Arts

Design Firm
Studio On Fire

St. Paul Minnesota 800 224 1536 **college of visual arts** cva.edu

COLLEGE OF VISUAL ARTS // SAINT PAUL, MINNESOTA // CVA.EDU // DESIGN: STUDIO ON FIRE (ALUMNI 1998)

College of Visual Arts // Saint Paul, Minnesota // CVA.EDU

Visual Poster, Versions 2 & 3

Client
College of Visual Arts

Design Firm
Studio On Fire

Unplug Poster

Client & Design Firm
Studio On Fire

UNPLUG
& GET YOUR
HANDS
DIRTY

THINKTOPIA®

Skull Poster

Client
Thinktopia

Copywriting
Patrick Hanlon

Design Firm
Studio On Fire

Illustration
Federico Jordan

Creative Direction
Patrick Hanlon

Studio On Fire Deskline

Design Firm
Studio On Fire

Design
Kelly English & Kindra Murphy

2007 Studio On Fire Letterpress Calendar

Design Firm
Studio On Fire

Illustration
Studio On Fire, Colorblok,
Brian Gunderson,
Rilla Alexander (Rinzen),
Plain Gravy, Faile

2008 Studio On Fire Letterpress Calendar

Design Firm
Studio On Fire

Illustration
Studio On Fire, Colorblok,
Brian Gunderson,
Rilla Alexander (Rinzen),
Justin Blythe, Harmen Liemburg

2009 Studio On Fire Letterpress Calendar

Design Firm
Studio On Fire

Illustration
Gunderson Jacobs,
Rilla Alexander (Rinzen),
Clarimus, Justin Blyth,
Adam Garcia, Studio On Fire

2010 Studio On Fire Letterpress Calendar

Design Firm
Studio On Fire

Illustration
Studio On Fire, Cecilie Ellefsen,
Brian Gunderson, The Little Friends
of Printmaking, ghostpatrol,
Rilla Alexander (Rinzen)

2011 Studio On Fire
Letterpress Calendar

Design Firm
Studio On Fire

Illustration
Studio On Fire,
Adam Garcia,
Brian Gunderson,
Jessica Hische,
We Make It So,
Aesthetic Apparatus

A LOVER NOT A FIGHTER

Jan / 11   Sun

Feb / 11   Sun

6
13
20
2

Dec / 11

	Sun	Mon	Tue	Wed	Thu	Fri	Sat
						1	2	3
					8	9	10
				7	14	15	16	17
	4	5	6	13	21	22	23	24
	11	12	20	28	29	30	31
	18	19	27				
	25	26					

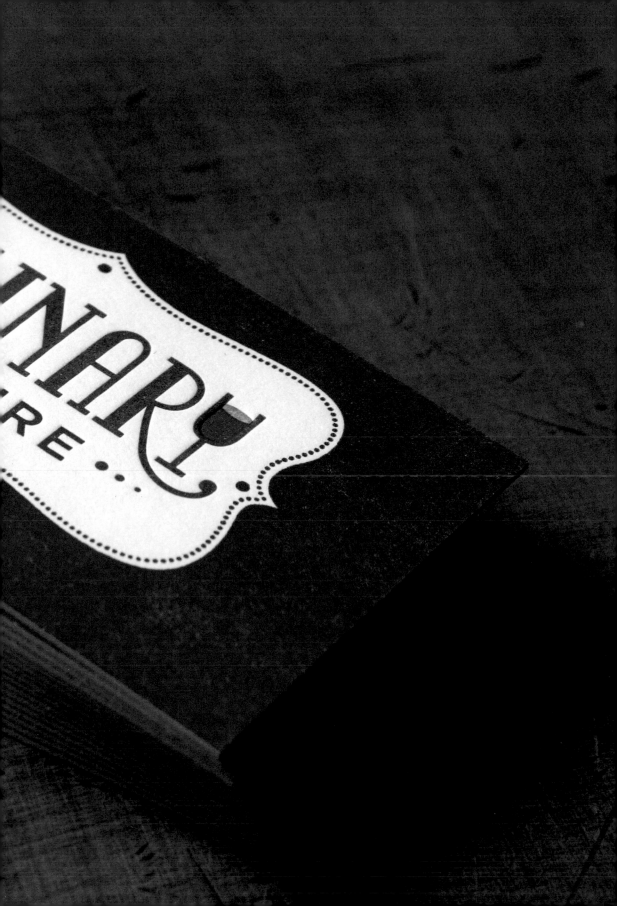

Culinary Culture Business Cards

Client
Culinary Culture/Mischa DeHart

Design
Jessica Hische

Holmberg Design Co. Business Cards

Client
Holmberg Design Co.

Design
Jeff Holmberg

HOLMBERG DESIGN CO.

JEFF HOLMBERG

6122296618

JEFF@HOLMBERGDESIGN.COM

HOLMBERGDESIGN.COM

H·DCO

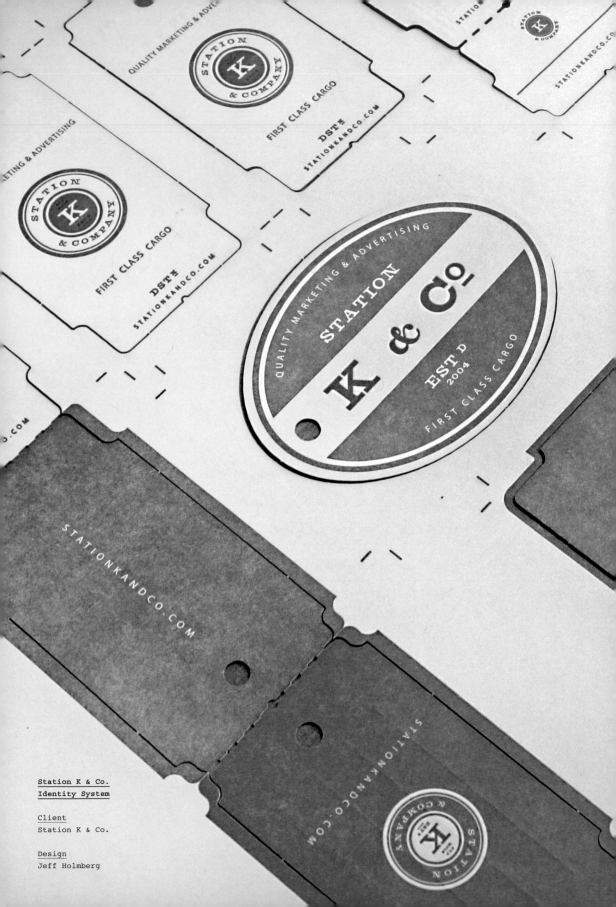

Station K & Co.
Identity System

Client
Station K & Co.

Design
Jeff Holmberg

Artistaday.com Business Cards

Client
Artistaday.com

Design
David Pitman

Others
485, inc

Dita Eyeware Business Cards

Client
Dita Eyeware

Design
Bryan Crabtree

Humanhand Business Cards

Client & Design Firm
Humanhand

Creative Direction
Justin Cravalho, Warren Daubert

Design
Justin Cravalho

Villainy and Associates Business Cards

Client & Design Firm
Villainy and Associates

Aphrochic

Client
Aphrochic

Design Firm
Passing Notes

Design
Abbie Planas Gong

Culinaria

Client
Culinaria

Design Firm
BiKlops Design

Design
Jeffrey Blake

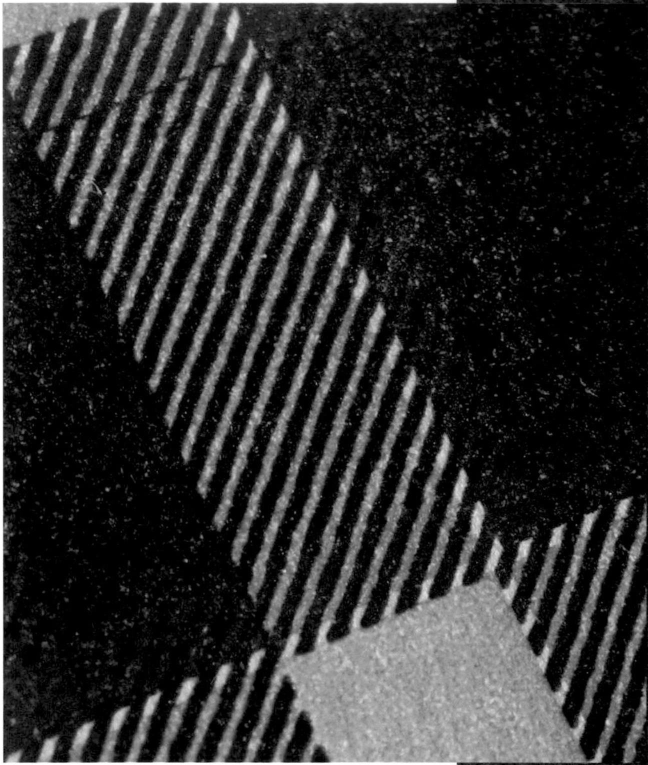

Mark Saunders | C

Mark Saunders | Creati

Mark Sa

Plaid Business Cards

Client & Design Firm
The Plaid Lab

Design
Mark Saunders

Director, Designer | 612 414 5957 | inquire@plaidlab.org

Mark Saunders | Creative Director, Designer | 612 414 5957 | inquire@plaidlab.org

ctor, Designer | 612 414 5957 | inquire@plaidlab.org

Creative Director, Designer | 612 414 5957 | inquire@plaidlab.org

Olli Salumeria Business Cards

Client
Olli Salumeria Americana, LLC

Design Firm
Miller Creative

Creative Direction
Reuben Miller

Art Direction
Yael Miller

Design
Yael Miller

Artist
Roger Xavier

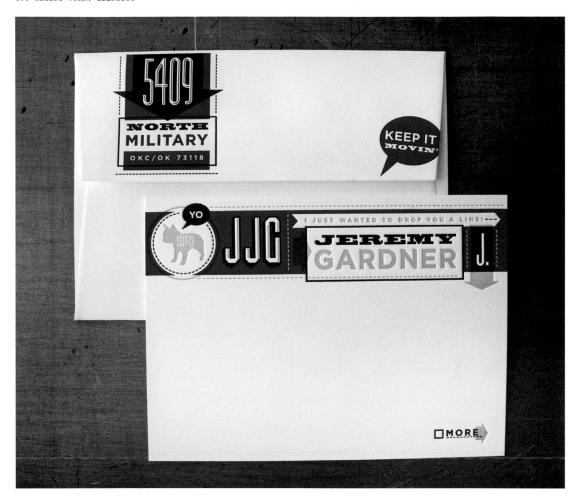

Jeremy Gardner Stationery

Client
Jeremy Gardner

Design
Mauricio Cremer

Others
Signal Creative

My Old Red Hat Business Cards

Client & Design Firm
My Old Red Hat

Design
Scott Ray

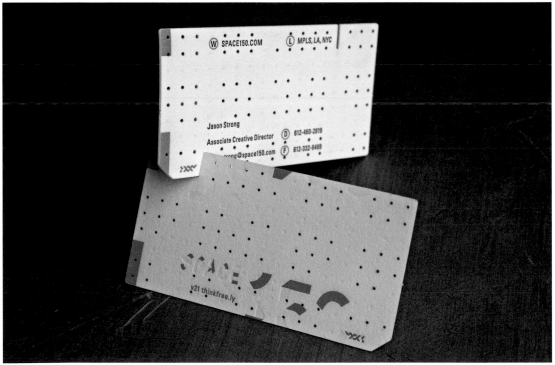

Welcome to Futurarium (space150 version 20)

Client & Design Firm	Copywriting
space150	Dane Roberts

Creative Direction	Design
ECD: William Jurewicz, Jason Strong	Ned Wright

thinkfree.ly (space150 version 21)

Client & Design Firm	Copywriting
space150	Dane Roberts

Creative Direction	Design
ECD: William Jurewicz, Jarrod Riddle	Ned Wright

Step Forward (space150 version 22)

Client & Design Firm   Design
space150   Dan Jenstad

Creative Direction
ECD: William Jurewicz

Copywriting
Michelle Swanson

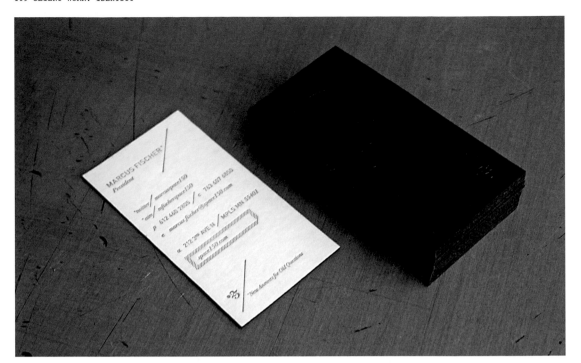

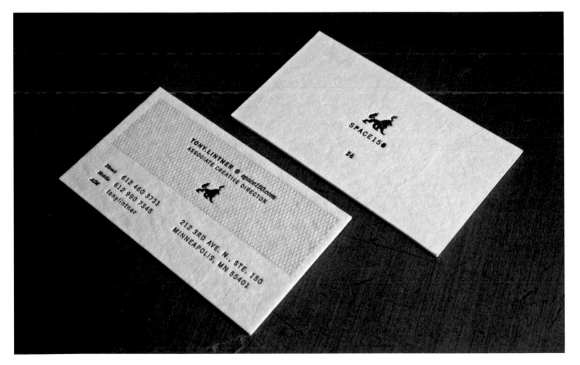

New Answers for Old Questions (space150 version 23)		Be Bold: Reinvent (space150 version 24)	
Client & Design Firm	**Copywriting**	**Client & Design Firm**	**Copywriting**
space150	Dane Roberts	space150	Ben Drake
Creative Direction	**Design**	**Creative Direction**	**Design**
ECD: William Jurewicz, Mike Fetrow	Ned Wright	ECD: William Jurewicz, Mike Fetrow	Ollie Bauer
	Strategist		
	Paul Isakson		

Ideas are Awesome (space150 version 25

Client & Design Firm
space150

Creative Direction
ECD: William Jurewicz,
Mike Fetrow

Design & Copywriting
Evan Nagan

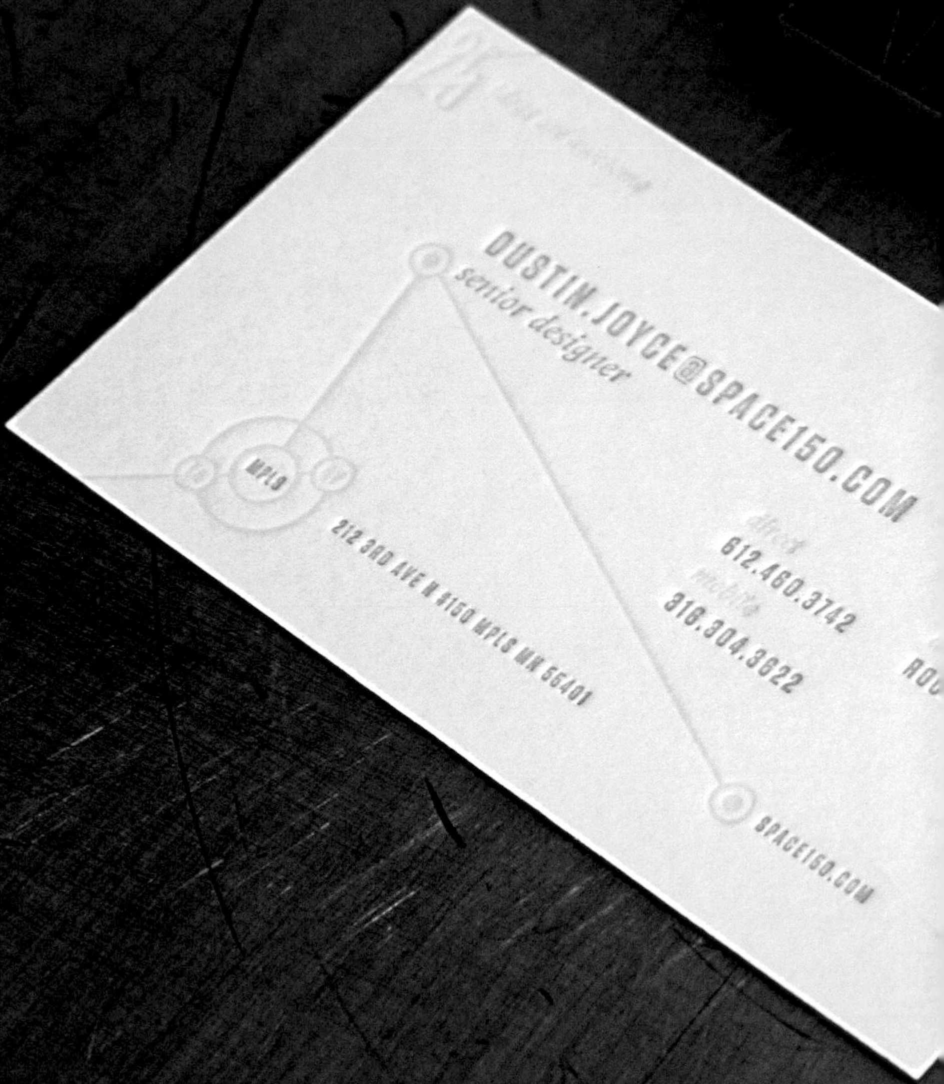

DUSTIN.JOYCE@SPACE150.COM
senior designer

MPLS

212 3RD AVE N #150 MPLS MN 55401

direct
612.460.3742
mobile
316.304.3622

ROU

SPACE150.COM

Born Revolvers (space150 version 26)

Client & Design Firm	Art Direction	Design
space150	Dustin Joyce	Dustin Sparks, Kari Anderson, Michael Watson, Matt Kuglitsch, Roven Bashier, Daniel Hennessy

Creative Direction	Copywriting	
ECD: William Jurewicz, Ned Wright	Cassie Broeckert, Michelle Swanson, Ben Drake, Todd Lintner	

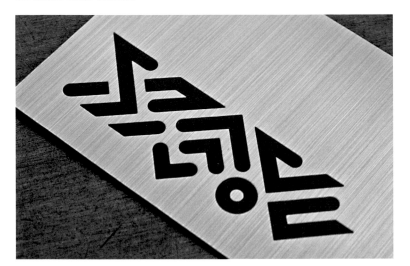

What If ... (space150 version 27)

Client & Design Firm	Art Direction	Design
space150	Michael Seitz	Andrew Ridgeway, Ben Olsem, Taylor Pemberton, Matt Kuglitsch

Creative Direction	Copywriting
ECD: William Jurewicz, Ned Wright	Jon Resheske

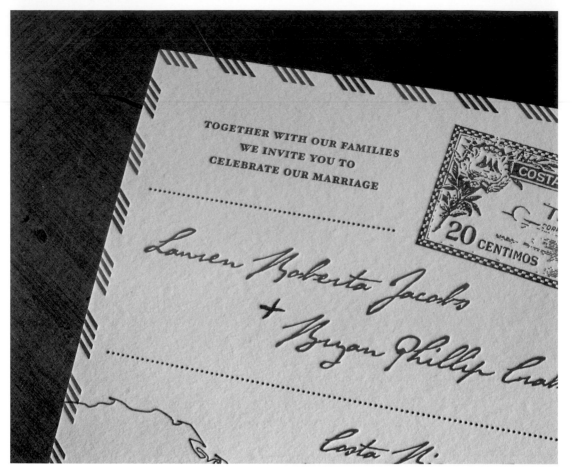

Costa Rica Wedding Invite

Client
Lauren & Bryan

Design
Bryan Crabtree

—THINGS TO KNOW—

revew.

VASANT AND SARLA TANK
&
ASHOK AND SHEELA MANTRI

invite you to celebrate the marriage
of their son and daughter,

Vikram & ...

SATURDAY, THE ...
TWO ...
AT FOUR ...
BARA ...

WITH BLESSINGS FROM
The Tank Family

Paternal Grandparents
PURSHOTTAM KANJIBHAI TANK (L)
LEELAVATI TANK (L)

Maternal Grandparents
MOHANLAL SOLANKI
LAXMIBEN SOLANKI

Paternal Uncles
GUNWANTRAI TANK (L)
RANJIT TANK

WITH BLESSINGS FROM
The Mantri Family

Paternal Grandparents
SHANKERRAO MANTRI (r.)
SAROJINI MANTRI (l.)

Maternal Grandparents
PRABHAKAR DESAI (r.)
SUNITA DESAI (l.)

With Best Compliments From
RESHAM MANTRI
ANGUS MACDONALD
MIRA MACDONALD

... OF MAY
... EN
... AFTERNOON.
... ALF PAST THREE.

...olly Hedge Estate
6987 UPPER YORK ROAD
NEW HOPE, PENNSYLVANIA 18938

~ dinner & dancing to follow ~

Vikram & Maya's Wedding
Invitation Suite

Client
Vikram Tank &
Maya Mantri

Design Firm
Pomegranita

Design
Priya Patel

ॐ

VASANT AND SARLA TANK
&
ASHOK AND SHEELA MANTRI
*invite you to celebrate the marriage
of their son and daughter,*

Vikram & Maya

SATURDAY, THE TWENTY-EIGHTH OF MAY
TWO THOUSAND ELEVEN
AT FOUR O'CLOCK IN THE AFTERNOON.
BARAAT BEGINS AT HALF PAST THREE.

Holly Hedge Estate
6987 UPPER YORK ROAD
NEW HOPE, PENNSYLVANIA 18938
~ dinner & dancing to follow ~

THINGS TO KNOW

WE HAVE RESERVED——SEATS
FOR YOU. KINDLY RSVP BY
MAY 1, 2011 BY VISITING
www.vikramandmaya.com

ULE OF EVENTS

a & Raas, 7:00PM
ETH AVENUE FIRE COMPANY
S AT HOLLY HEDGE ESTATE
:30PM
DRIVEWAY
:0PM
RD
:0PM

Vikram &
Maya Tank

Nichole & Tim's Wedding Invitations

Client
Nichole & Tim Michel

Design Firm
Coral Pheasant Stationery + Design

Marci & Ben's Wedding Invitations

Client
Marci DeLozier & Benjamin Haas

Design
Erin Jang/The Indigo Bunting

PLEASE JOIN US in CELEBRATING THE UNION OF MARGARET MCGEE and CONN NEWTON

October 16th, 2010 — 12 PM

AT THE BASILICA OF SAINT MARY

88 Seventeenth Street North
Minneapolis, Minnesota 55403

RECEPTION TO FOLLOW

AT PATRICIA NEWTON'S RESIDENCE — 3:30 PM

3580 NORTHOME
DEEPHAVEN

Margaret & Conn's Wedding Invitations

Client
Conn Newton & Margie McGee

Copywriting
Conn Newton

Design
Anchalee Chambundabongse

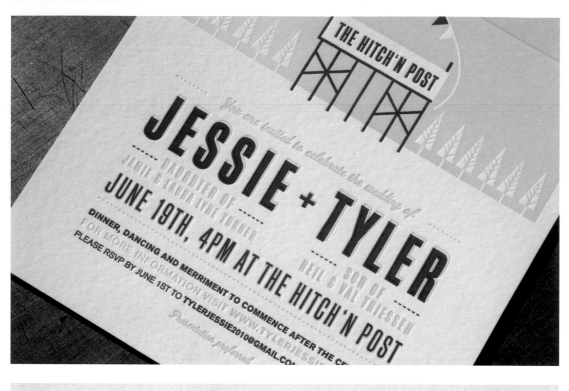

Jessie & Tyler's Wedding Invitations

Client
Tyler & Jessie Thiessen

Design Firm
One Plus One Design

Design
Tyler & Jessie Thiessen

Kathleen & William's Wedding Invitations

Client
Kathleen K. Peiffer

Creative Direction
Kathleen Peiffer, Scott Peiffer

Design
Scott Peiffer

Bahamas Wedding Party Invitations

Client
Kathleen K. Peiffer

Creative Direction
Kathleen Peiffer, Scott Peiffer

Design
Scott Peiffer

Monica & Nathan

BECAUSE YOU HAVE SHARED IN OUR LIVES BY YOUR FRIENDSHIP & LOVE, WE

Monica A. Jaramillo & Nathan R. L...

TOGETHER WITH OUR FAMILIES
INVITE YOU TO CELEBRATE THE BEGINNING OF OUR NEW LIFE TO...
ON SATURDAY, THE TWENTY-FIFTH OF JUNE
TWO THOUSAND ELEVEN
AT FIVE O'CLOCK IN THE EVENING
AMERICAS SOCIETY · 680 PARK AVENU...
NEW YORK CITY
RECEPTION TO FOLLOW
BLACK TIE OPTIONAL

PLEASE SAVE THE DATE FOR THE WED...
MONICA JARAMILLO &...
JUNE 25, 2011 ·
FORMAL INVITATION TO FOL...

Monica & Nate's Wedding Invitations

Client
Monica & Nate

Design Firm
Pomegranita

Design
Priya Patel

MONICA & NATHAN

First Course Trio

SALAD OF MIXED BABY FIELD GREENS
TOSSED WITH A BALSAMIC VINAIGRETTE

MARINATED OLIVES

MURCIA AL VINO CHEESE
QUINCE PASTE AND A PLANTAIN CHIP

Choice of Entrée

INDIVIDUAL PEPPER CRUSTED FILET OF BEEF
BRUSHED WITH CHIMMICHURRI
ROASTED FINGERLING POTATOES WITH OLIVES, TOMATOES,
PEPPERS & CARAMELIZED ONIONS

PAN ROASTED CILANTRO PESTO STRIPED BASS
TOMATILLO SALSA, STICKY RICE CAKE TRIANGLE AND
BUNDLED VEGETABLES

Dessert

TRIO OF SORBETS
COCONUT, PASSION FRUIT, MANGO
WITH RASPBERRY SAUCE DRIZZLE

RATION OF

AN LANDER

K CITY
LANDMONICA.COM

THE FAVOR OF YOUR REPLY IS REQUESTED BY MAY FIRST

M

○ ACCEPTS WITH PLEASURE

○ DECLINES WITH REGRETS

Mariko & Mark's Wedding Invitations

Client
Mariko & Mark

Design
Julia Kostreva

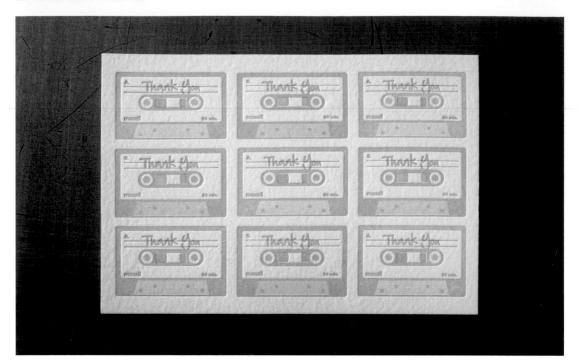

Micah & Ruth's Wedding Invitations

Client
Micah & Ruth Pertersen

Design
Adam Ramreth

A+D Wedding Invitations

Client
Self-Promotion

Design
Drew Hodgson

Shepard Mattson Birth Announcements

Client
Shepard Mattson

Design Firm
Mattson Creative

Design
Ty Mattson

Infinite Possibilities

Client & Design Firm
Eight Hour Day

Creative Direction
Katie Kirk, Nathan Strandberg

Design
Nathan Strandberg

Let's tell **BETTER STORIES**

Here's a little something we made in our spare time.

Enjoy!

winkinc.com

Swink Campfire

Client & Design Firm
Swink

Art Direction
Drew Garza,
Yogie Jacala

Creative Direction
Shanan Galligan

Field Guide for the Target Chalet

Client & Design Firm
Target

Copywriting
Jeff Barbian

Creative Direction
Phil Clark, Aaron Melander

Design
Aaron Melander

Art Direction
Aaron Melander

DOGWOOD

COFFEE CO.

COUNTRY

COLOMBIA
RIO NEGRO MICROLOT
MPLS MN USA

NAME

Dogwood Coffee Co. Coffee Labels

Client
Dogwood Coffee Co.

Design
Jeff Holmberg

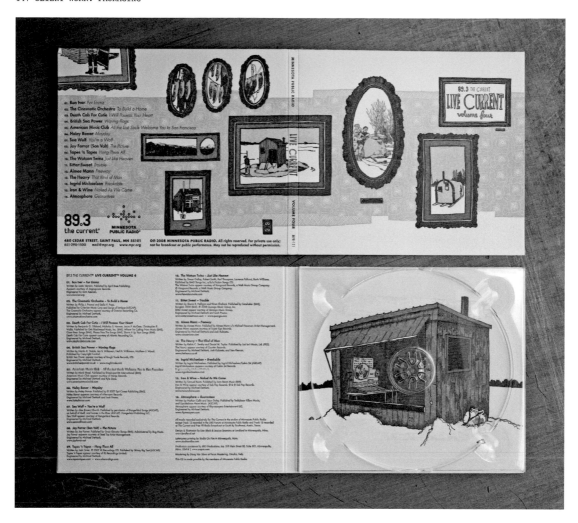

Live Current Vol. 4

Client
Minnesota Public Radio/The Current

Design Firm
Landland

Design
Dan Black, Jessica Seamans

Illustration
Jessica Seamans

Douglas Quin: Fathom LP

Client
TAIGA records

Copywriting
René van Peer

Design Firm
Loaf Nest

Design
Loaf Nest

Creative Direction
Andrew Lange, Douglas Quin

Drawings
Mitchell Dose

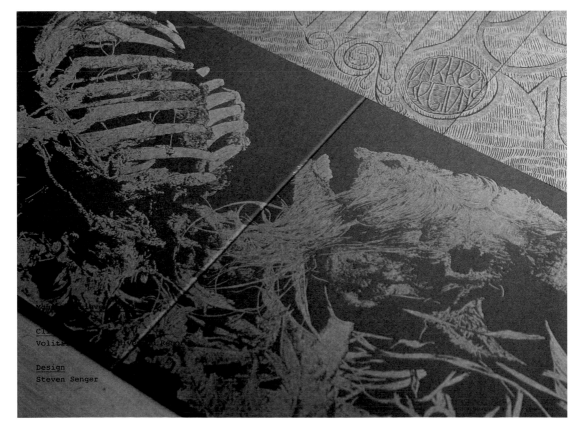

Material
Client
Voliti... ...live and Recor...

Design
Steven Senger

Knife Wrap

Client & Design Firm
Shine Advertising

Copywriting
James Breen

Creative Direction
Mike Kriefski

Design
Chad Bollenbach

Art Direction
John Krull

Flashlight Wrap

Client & Design Firm
Shine Advertising

Copywriting
James Breen

Creative Direction
Mike Kriefski

Design
Chad Bollenbach

Art Direction
John Krull

Office Print

Client & Design Firm
Eight Hour Day

Creative Direction
Katie Kirk, Nathan Strandberg

Design
Katie Kirk

Thought & Motion Poster

Client
University of Minnesota Dance

Design Firm
Spunk Design Machine

Creative Direction
Jeffrey Johnson, Ben Pagel

Copywriting
Ben Pagel

Design & Illustration
Justin Martinez

The Great Gatsby Business Card Poster

Client & Design Firm
The Heads of State

Creative Direction
Jason Kernevich

Copywriting
F. Scott Fitzgerald,
Jason Kernevich

Design
Jason Kernevich,
Raphael Geroni

MY PRESS IS HUMAN, EVEN AS I,

BECAUSE IT IS MY LIFE.

THUS, I WILL LEARN IT AS A BROTHER.

I WILL LEARN ITS WEAKNESSES,

ITS STRENGTHS, ITS PARTS,

ITS ACCESSORIES, ITS GEARS

AND ITS LUBRICATION SCHEDULE.

I WILL EVER OIL AND GREASE IT

AGAINST THE RAVAGES OF DAMAGE

AS I WILL EVER GUARD MY ARMS,

MY HANDS AND FINGERS AGAINST DAMAGE.

I WILL KEEP MY PRESS

CLEAN AND READY.

WE WILL BECOME

PART OF EACH OTHER.

WE WILL ...

BEFORE GOD, I SWEAR THIS CREED.

MY PRESS AND MYSELF

ARE THE CRAFTSMEN OF GOOD DESIGN.

WE ARE THE MASTERS OF COLOR.

WE ARE THE MAKERS

OF THE CREATIVE INDUSTRY.

SO BE IT, UNTIL

ALL THE PAPER IS TRIMMED

AND MY PRESS IS READY

FOR THE NEXT PIECE!

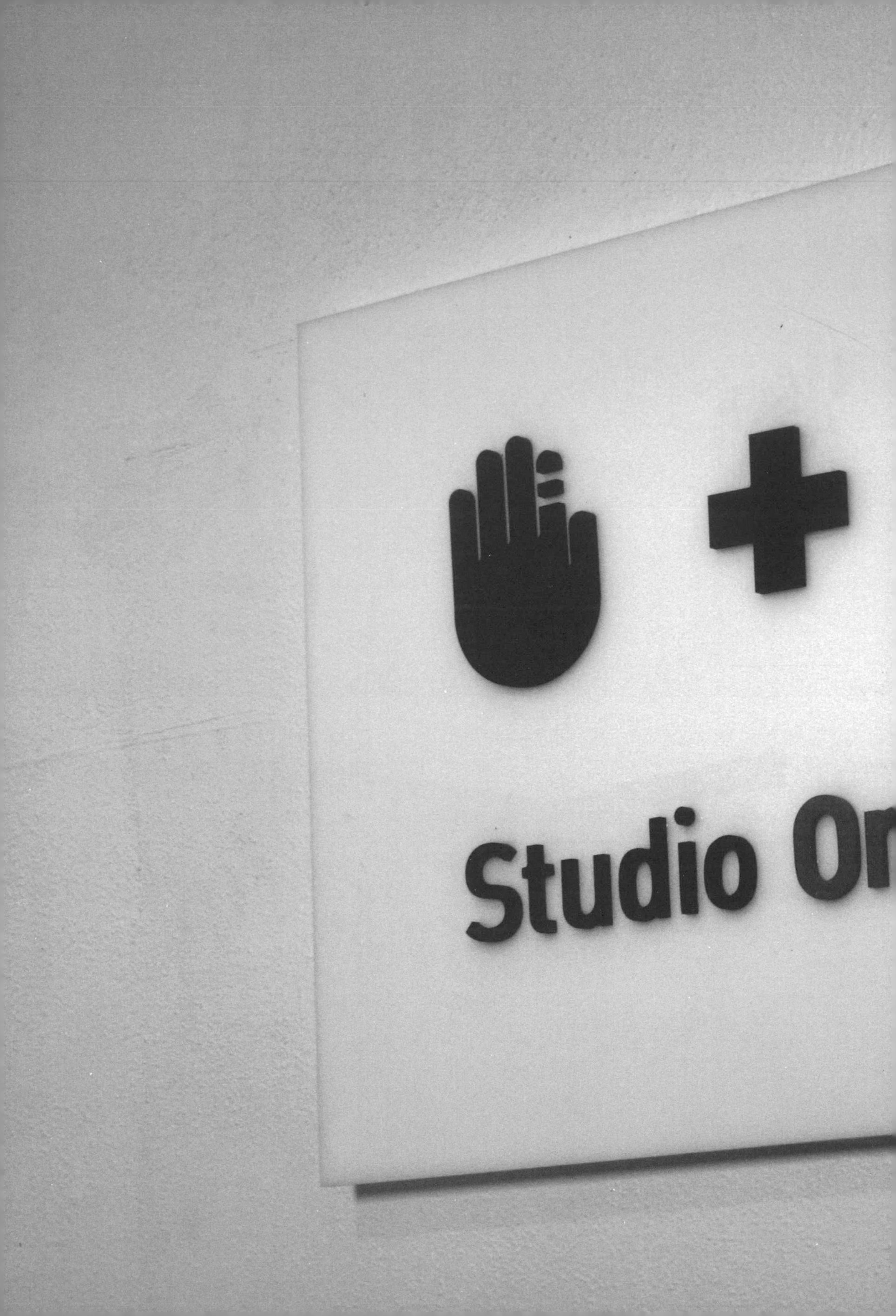
Studio